In My Best Voice

NEW AND SELECTED POEMS

Mary Virginia Micka

YTTERLI PRESS

2005

ACKNOWLEDGMENTS

Certain of these poems, some in slightly different versions, first appeared in *The National Catholic Reporter*, *The New Yorker*, *Southern Poetry Review*, *WARM Journal*, *Border Crossings, an Anthology* (St. Paul: New Rivers Press, 1984), *Three Bridges* (Omaha: Lone Willow Press, 2002), and in a series of chapbooks and audiocassettes self-published in 1987–1997, the most recent of which, *Distances*, under the auspices of Wisdom Ways, St. Paul.

I extend special thanks to the Leadership Team and Community members of the Sisters of St. Joseph of Carondelet, St. Paul Province; and also to Ruth Brombach and the Alumnae Association of the College of St. Catherine; Robert Grunst; Deborah Keenan; Mary E Kraft, CSJ; Kerin McTeigue; Pat and Buzz Myser; Yvette Nelson; Mary Rose O'Reilley; Sylvia Ruud; Magdalen Schimanski, CSJ; and Fredrick Zydek.

Library of Congress Catalog Card Number applied for.

Printed in the United States of America.

Published by Ytterli Press
2211 Buford Avenue, St. Paul MN 55108

Book design by Sylvia Ruud

Drawings by Mary Virginia Micka

To everyone and everything in my world.

CONTENTS

I. All I Can Do

II. *This Swaying Web*

III. Scorched Season

IV. The Turning Page

In My Best Voice

IN MY BEST VOICE

Then there's this pile
of my various utterances,
some of which I've decided
are priceless

precisely because now and then
one will really act like an utterance,
i.e., when I say it aloud to myself
in my best voice, it resounds,
sometimes twice, filling the whole space
even if at the time I can't remember
ever before having said anything like that
to anyone.

Except, of course, God.

Which in my book
goes without saying.

As for the rest of the pile,
that's priceless, too,
come to think of it,
in ways crying out to be
dealt with directly.

Which I will do.

I.

All I Can Do

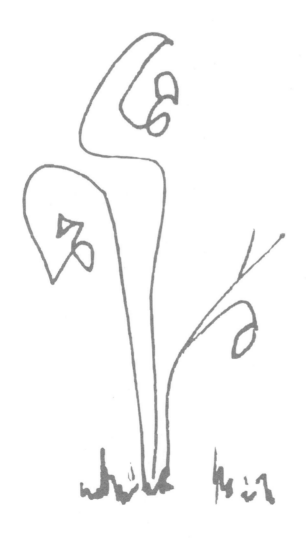

How, When the Muse?

You
look up at me
from the page, in at me
from my window day
or night, out at me
from my heart: I pretend
I can see you.

What, when you finally
come, will I do
first? Bid my hands fly?
Cry your name? Whisper,
breathe mine? Or remember
all I can do, really,
is yes?

THESE
AND LIKE QUESTIONS

Who owns the dark?

Who wraps
sleeper with thief sped,
my life in his sack?

Who steals in the jungle,

moves forward then back
into shadow, becoming
the shadow? Who

ripens dreams caught in branches
we thought no longer fruitful?

Who takes this delight?

Who under the sea
bids the anemone turn
blushing and golden
designs for her unhurried kingdom?

Who is sighing?

Who is bending and stumbling? Are there
old recipes we have forgotten?

How much must we try to remember?

Will God ever sing
so we can hear? A glee or catch
sweeping light over the meadow?

How can we discover what we own?
Is somewhere the first
saying or garden still growing?

Is there a rising of love swifter
than the most hurtful thing we can imagine?

Who under or within hastens
our configurations with ease?

What is all
to the mole or the owl, to the slow-
singing anemone?

If there is all, why these
snatches and crumbs?

Who is sighing?

Does God sing?

DARE EVERYTHING

Dare everything. See how
even the stripped elm,

having learned
angels are not liable to death
nor was the bush consumed, only
burned that place holy,

glows now down its branches.

Undo, then,
from the sweet body of earth
everything, male and female, everything
but the fire: then dare death
grave us in ice.

IN A SEASON OF RAIN

In a season of rain
a stranger in mackintosh
hums to himself on his dogged way
around the pond. He will
reappear, hound at his heels,
out of the green mist.

Someone I remember
whose hand on my shoulder
a long time ago knew
neither first word nor last, only
a music, a song circling.

BECAUSE IN NOTHING

Because in nothing
are you quite
still or sure, I
watch for you in
spaces between, as
between heartbeats, where
nothing is happening,

where silence, like distance,
lies tangled in strumming
of lutes, lyres
bidding the blood
pour out, if only it could,
blossoms of extravagant glory

as if unaware
all one can utter burns
in a silence of stars watching.

Before the Icon

Not today, Mother of God, not
today, your serene face in shadow,
present me no Child.

                No,
that Spirit at her loom
weaving a year and a day
into star-flowers like eyes
waking under their lashes,
                      beckon her:
bid her catch me up, too,
thread my blood's run
through every flung field of this earth,
caverns and deltas and piled towers
on and on and all languages, their vast
power, yes, to deny.

MY MOTHER SANG

My mother sang at her stove.
This kettle and that
whistled and bounced
at the boil. Listening
as her long spoon dipped
and circled, I learned
of a little brown bird
that sang, too, in the hush
of the darkness and the dew. I buried
my nose in the fragrance of her arm
and from that deep place watched
how the nest rocked
but the brown bird, yes, sang on
through the dark hush all night long
until morning, when arm in arm
we would step out past the tulips
still pink with sleep but
nodding as we passed, she
now in her dainty dress and I
keeping her careful company, both
guessing who it might be this time
waiting for us in the shadow
of the willow tree. And we
grew together that way.

Once Having Left a Long-Loved Place

There
nothing's lost: hills
hug their very scars, weeds cling
and crickets won't let go,
hydrangeas tough with grace
bind root to autumn
and the great span of stars.

Once, being there slipped like all things lost
into the slot of dreams. There
I go looking sometimes in the night,
but it refuses me.

lost until found

my umbrella my bathrobe were hers

yesterday the umbrella fell away
secretly   climbing the bus
something at my arm missing
that windbreak rainbreak   well
now it's time   go on
without it

then out of dark sleep to cry
mother   o mother   see
crowds of us
deep drenched in
too soon not knowing

your shade shelter
slips all untimely no matter when/
where all of us

in our pain then   patience   listen
o mother   your soft
sleeve still cover us until
sunbreak

SEASONAL

Leaves drop one by one. Gulls
lift and circle the water.

Still as thought, red berries
step away from their shells.

Old crow rattles his branch
at every head passing beneath him.

Snow steals, barely a whisper,
over the yard. We watch quiet as trees.

My world, white and wide. No word
but casts a shadow.

Snow drifting and, some nights,
stars. Steady my cold heart.

Clouds burst, flooding your garden.
Forgive me.

A Great Snow Falling

Wide night glistens
like coal and my window a black
square of snowing, each flake a word.
Neither hurry nor sound, only
somewhere out there one wolf poised
between trees, yellow eye
gathering plans. And I nameless
wordless mere downslide of feather
melting in air. So much unwritten.

Against darkness a white breath
against glass.

So much unwritten: *love* and *death*
two words breathed, glistening the dark.

High wind pulls at smoke rising from chimneys.
Such cold. Hide from as it were God
sweeping a steely glance, remember
hearth fires ablaze, the expansive free
utterly summer-solstice of love.

Who said love is warm? Love is a steel shaft
burning and cutting. Take no particular comfort
in what love does: strew flowers, speed/shatter
the blood, bump us into each other by sheer chance
as we head full steam from opposite directions
toward the same red apple in the bowl, then
call out Stop Right There

let one recognition and another
drift into being and maintain itself mid-air
without hurry or sound until at your least nod
it moves, if perhaps shyly, to a spot
nearer the fire.

Love calls for this,
day and night pacing the floor even of dreams
in search of herself, pausing now at my window
with a third word, larger than air, *yes*.

I KNOW SOME SCIENTIFIC TERMS

I know some scientific terms
for things and happenings and even
use a few to edify myself
if I remember. But all's forgot
when clouds whipped white
as cream on top drag in a leaden load
to dump on us: I simply see
a coming dark, feel coming cold and, inexplicably,
some holy mystery of love.

Such fond language as that last
lives in me where I neither speak
nor understand. But there it is, in terms today
of snowflakes drifting down through empty air
to find my cheek or side by side lay intricacies
against my sleeve. I go in lace.

And not alone: a child stops midway, waits
until one cool surprise
reaches her outstretched palm, then
stumbles with delight
to catch another on her tongue.

MY UNCLE BIRD

Like on every other morning, he was whistling
in the cornfield for his friend, a neighbor at her window
said. His blue shirt just sank down among the leaves.
They rustled some, then settled back. Such a bright sky.

That was his passage.

*

My Uncle Bird sang like his name high in the choir
Christmas mornings. Waiting at home with my doll,
I saw his face lifted into the light
of some great window. Yes we must wait.
When there he stood, rosy with smiles, at the door,
we curled our toes tight across the tops
of his holiday shoes and rode back in, he still,
and all of us now, singing.

My Uncle Bird, fatherless, cast off by wife and
children as way too tender, could not after that
find even God the Father, only his own shame or sorrow,
whatever it was that set him baking cookies—wreaths
and Santas, trees and stars lined up for folks
still willing to help themselves to his life.
One blurred October photo shows the trays already
heaped with that year's offerings of frostings, flutings,
puffs and pockets, scatters of red and green dots.
And sure enough they came, airmail, at Christmas,
a box of hard crumbles tumbling out,
God the Mother singing the bright morning.

UNDER A WILD SKY

Under a wild sky, wild
and vacant as a cry,
I walk the frozen stubble,
mouse, cricket long since gone.

My cat against my ankle lets me know
she too has courage. I pick her up
and tuck her in along my jacket
sleeve. I touch her ear.

We stand alone in time

and then turn back to where an hour ago
she'd watched me lay our evening fire.

Even Now Sometimes

Even now sometimes
I mix You up with my father in his chair
reading under the lamp, me
putting my four dolls to sleep
one by one,
humming and hushing them down
around his big shoes.

Then this idea would come: they can just
take care of themselves for a while,

and I'd crawl closer to lean my own head
against where the wool folded in soft
at the bend of his knee, knowing
if I sat there still enough
and long enough with my eyes closed,
a cap of warm fingers would come settle
on my hair, then curve down to fit
over my ears in case I was cold—
at least, that's how I remember it.

What I Like

I like when
you lean down
(I suppose)
and kiss me
on top of my head.
It makes a
warm spot where
the part is.
I sit up straight
for days and
get things done.
Where did you
learn that
about me? Where
do you go?

THIS SENTENCE

The patch on my ceiling waits like an eyelid
to see
what will come of this sentence.

True, four or five pieces of glass
dangle in air, but their touchings
are scarcely a sentence.

One crow sets his syllables out, two
only. I picture them black.
The third is an echo.

Miles up, the air has no trouble at all
lifting the airplane. This implies
somebody's work is driving ahead with terrible speed.

A list of things brought to a halt
could go on for hours. It might include
sports cars gaping in heaps,
clogged bobbins, prayers
caught in the throat,
left boot, right boot,
any shell, socket, clean bone
remaining. These
modify nothing.

All solids melted together make the great sea
of liquids and gasses coming and going
so that from birth to death
the child at the shore must be looking for objects:

this grapefruit whole, then halved,
this sunflower in rags bending
into the honey, holy St. Mary from her bright
metal medallion noticing all
rounds returning.

STARING

I stare at
my philodendron's
green wealth,
how it thrives
on no sun at all
and my mother
with her begonias
luscious orange
in north shade
and right there
get caught in
my line of thought
and can't talk.

OLD WOMEN

These old women hang on
in the face of all that persists,
even when all that persists is bone,
lean, shattered or polished to death.
They get up every day, these women,
face the sharp lens of it,
startle even the box held otherwise lax
to the heart of an otherwise stranger.

Then their faces come home,
get out of cameras and into collections—
I have at least seven, the most recent
being this old woman from India
wrinkled as string:
her mouth and eyes know me without mercy
but steady and sure all the same
there persists a great womb
greater than ocean, with seed
growing into every possible space
and will not in any way
be shattered to death. She says
I should believe her.

CHOPIN ON THE ST. CROIX

Everything,
even landscape,
slides away with the river
unless event center it.
Event for its center
has person and moment:

                 the man
playing this Etude, say, and
the listener
watching the river
sliding away until now.

It Would Seem

Hand and tongue
being finite
can at this hour
only desire

as must the Infinite
it would seem,
having once chosen
to weave Itself

throb by throb
into our longing.

WAKING IN AIR

Someone in the white village this morning
early, without thinking,
ripples a scarf of orange anemones
through the air. It will settle smooth
on a white table
                but the air
still floating flowers
sends someone next door smiling
deeper into her dream
                    of a third neighbor now
descending his stair and pausing
to watch shawl upon shawl of new snow sinking
over the field.
              So vast this
extension of sleep, he must
blink away dark when
at the field's far edge a lone skier, orange
and black in the distance, blooms
on the trackless space; yet
                    once he is certain
color is waking the air,
then, wanting breakfast,
                the sleeper
will open her eyes.

In Absentia

In my photograph of two people on a faraway couch
you are looking at me across light
and I am looking at everything to be learned
from one moment, i.e.,
how ash from a person's cigar could drop even now
into his open palm—a person should notice, be more careful
leaning like that; how shirt buttons—four,
and a fifth at the cuff—quicken
in lamp glow; how the ear waits; how everywhere
there must be watches—little gleams as the wrist turns,
yours or mine; how already it is the future, yet
much is unseen; how the tongue
in mid-syllable stops.
                    Which is why
the other person, the one you looked over at, can only stare out
holding onto her teacup with both hands while her hair
flies away and her eyes widen and the bright
hush of her dress goes on singing.

II.

This Swaying Web

OVERHEARD: #1

Thus spake the top:

You hear "strawberry" and right away
you naturally think "luscious!"
me meanwhile being shut up
in the drawer with all those erasers,
my five blue leaves and nine white spots
not being apparent.

Until that drawer gets opened—
for a casual look-see, I suppose—then, uh-oh,
there I am
lifted out into the light. But
by the warmest hand you could imagine.

Then, I don't know—
one flick of that wrist
and I get to go spinning away
like there's no tomorrow. Round and round
the whole scene just this morning,
right over a paper clip
if you can believe it, never missing a beat,
swear to God, it was glorious! like
whenever that flick happens,
I am something else, I can tell you!
Ask me anything / anything!
                              No.
Don't ask. I can't begin to say
what when where why, only that this WHO,
whoever, starts up such delight in me
I plan to spin on, give or take
a short rest now and then, forever.

In Season and Out

Think snow peas'
sweet snap
think lettuce leafy
low nest of sun
think carrots
cabbages tight-veined
bluish and crisp
then how parsley
spills a green spray
a moth visits
tangles of blossom and vine
where beans dangle
until you can reach them.

Ping plop rustle
a thud and your bucket
gets heavy you pull
with a grunt
and the garden
lets go of your shoes
you head for the house
trailing mud
breathing dill
blessing life all its shapes
its overnight sounds its
large and small labors
even to be.

THE BIRTHMARK

The girl with the long red
birthmark on her cheek
has written a poem about waking
in the white morning in a white room.

Yet how can I, as she would wish, blindly,
read line by line betraying
an innocent longing borne without reason
from the beginning—for the poem says
this is someone else's room that is so
white, this is not
her own room—or reach through this clear
syllabled window
to touch? Did she, I wonder,
once or twice in the writing touch
that alien pigment her mother would have felt
from the beginning?
                She writes
that in this white room she is proud
to be so white, so clean
it is impossible to feel guilty, telling me
only in lines lost or not written
what she would wish,
that we read not seeing her
waking or sleeping
outside her poem, in her own room
as if the pure, utterly white room
were not, for all of us, from the beginning,
someone else's white room.

PAS DE DEUX

Design and timing, an exquisite
execution of swift dance, and once again
the practiced mouse escapes. A dark
potato place she knows shapes her
a kind of sanctuary where
thanksgiving prayers
phrased to a narrow life swell now
beyond the interstices of her ribs until
they breathe above the mould
aureoles of inexhaustible sweet grace
to sing her home.

                And yet,
whose pleasure's this? Say
if you can
the cat's—still, inward,
burning toward his own design
of final seizure and deposit, thus:
        loop of a silver paw and on the carpet
        four pink feet gathered
        tight as rosebuds in a wreathing light.

OLD RIVER TOWN

On a shady street in the old river town
two young men work quietly
rebuilding an old house. Perhaps
as they lay eye, then nail
to the wood, they see their dream
caught out of the curling river
taking measure and shape, and tomorrow
their brushes heavy with white paint
will waken gable and newel
to many more winters. Yes, that is
their dream, it is easy to see
in their silence together as they move
back and forth through the hours
and the shadows rebuilding the house.

And it is permitted here. A sign on the door
says all this is permitted a quiet old
flowing-on town.

PAEAN

Houses: their skins, shells
open or not on chambers and juices.

As for pears—green yellow-green blush red-blush
crimson and overlays of the above—

pears have a long history although
shorter than houses, almost 2000 years,
beginning in bright blue Persia,
I have read. Charlemagne
on a day in late summer got hold of one,
its juice bellying to fullness at his teeth,
then bade his gardener plant
thousands of trees. Picture the belling!
Adroit poets did just that in paeans to pears,
rhyming Bartlett Anjou Bosc even Seckel
with language in high Holy Roman
for white smooth juicy sweet-to-very-sweet
even buttery, as these words came
consoling their tongues.

Another day in late summer the first
fruit-bowl display: bell-shaped
egg-shaped brown-skinned with tapering neck
squat almost round excellent poached pickled perhaps
glazed. Picture that mighty hand reached across
empire, its blue skies and palaces as well as
bodies in and out of squat houses, doors
open or not and chambers bellying fullness
ripe now for biting.

SUCH AS THESE

Even such as these
join the long line:

a boy
the boy on his knees
on his knees calling
to his cat caught
under a pipe
the cat caught
under a big pipe
the pipe

a boy on his knees crying

one by one
the still stars.

WHAT LESS THAN AIR

Your finger traveled down my cheek
to find my lip
was only that, no more
than its own weight.

It scarcely signifies.

And yet, what is it, almost daily,
less than air but deeper
than my life and yours together
cries out for recognition?

I kiss your moving finger, do not know.

THE POOR EYE

The eye
the poor blind eye
looks not for likeness (metaphor
is laughable in its un-
likeness), only the one word
for how all winds together
scour the sky clear of north/south cloud-runs
and then heave clumps of autumn
red-gold against it

so the eye works
angles, lengthens, negotiates curves
around bowl and drape, delves into layers,
lifts to follow where the lintel
cuts an oblong through paint—like a yawn,
is it? or cave? neither:
a door the color of chestnuts

registers parallels, in themselves and in
their double and quadruple uprights or slants
along book spines, pipes, and rods
in old-fashioned radiators deep-
pleated with inaccessible shadows; or across,
as in chair rungs or any one of seven possible
styles of molding

is caught without warning into loops, traceries,
filigrees, flutings, fresh spiderwebs taking the sun

furthermore,
works like this hours at a stretch, often past dark,
before closing down silent under its lid.

AFTER THE BIOPSY

At the end of the meal, still
attentive to hunger, embrace this woman
leaving her ripened fields. Return
her eyes to those delicate gardens
woven in birdsong, petal, and bee, spell
once more into her ear pod and gourd,
berry zinnia anything succulent
fragrant or gold, everything
rinsed with delight. She will hear
but turn from you—be prepared—and you
sit down again to the famine
of all mortal flesh crying after.

RECIPES

Sometimes, with everything
pouring or sifting into inevitable
transformations and me not ready,
I copy out recipes. These are
directions someone else has already
followed, so I'm sure enough
one cup of this measured against
five stirrings of that
will turn out right.
I can put together
Aunt Jewel's gingersnaps, Aunt Lula's
baked beans, my mother's pheasant
and coffee cake, even Mayme's pineapple torte,
though these women have long since
sifted away away down the world
still in its vast making.

Evenings and Sundays my mother
read new recipes
with an intensity I could not
understand except for their pictures,
luscious achievements on platters or
hugged comfortably into their bowls.
Or she would sort through her smudged
notebook, spreading things out
on a card table, then discarding or
copying over. Near the end
she cleaned out her recipe drawer
until all that remained were

absolute favorites
to hold our escaping life a while longer
by its seasons—chess pies and cranberry
pudding, Lady Baltimore cake once a year
for my father, strawberry jam
with the strawberries spread whole
under white cloths on the counter overnight
while we slept away summers.
By the time her cleaning was finished,
we could finally open the drawer without grunting
for a change, and close it again
without kicking, because
there was only that one big
book left, I remember.

I heard about a farm woman once
who made notes, some of them dated,
about just how it was
the day she cooked up a recipe. Right
on the card she drew the line of hills
or put down about the wolf tracks or Benny's
perpetual wheeze or
how the corn was beginning to come.
One note said that year they lost
all their grapes—I picture the leaves
shriveling back from her window—
and one said August wasn't a good month
for colds or to be using the oven.
A friend of mine found these recipes

at a flea market, the cards all yellowed
but the notes clear as the other ingredients.

Another friend is dying of cancer
and we feel around, trying
what to say to each other about that.
Yesterday, calm as anything,
she brought over her recipe box.

Some time is clear,
measured as much as you need
to make everything turn out right, but
when that goes, I look for more
recipes to copy.

RINSE O WHITE

When it says right here on the label
Do Not Bleach, what are you supposed to do,
for God's sake, about the spots? Beer and
salad dressing and look at all that cat
scat. What happens
when you bleach them anyway,
these polyester white-to-begin-with
stretch-to-your-shape pants
you were a fool to buy
in the first place? Well,
what? Do they end up
yellow? rot
from the inside out? slow-burn
through the cuff or in the pockets?

If so, then better go
with the spots, start with scrub
as much as possible between
your heavy-duty no-bleach raw
knuckles, imitating
the ritual of washboards and before that
beating until clean on
ancient rocks
and then when this
doesn't work, simply
kneel down in
maybe even the mud
in pure acknowledgement
to the manufacturer that as far as his
whites are concerned, you're out
beyond your depth.

HOW-TO

These how-to cookbooks, even
fancy French ones with pictures,
don't actually promise
you can do it yourself, e.g.,
boeuf en daube.

All the same, every household's
better off having at least one such
pictorial collection of impossible
achievements, e.g., pink
frosting in peaks, glazed carrot
and onion side by side with tomato
catching the light, ruffles, no dust,
white cat tucked in prettily to approve
this whole spread of left-handed re-
minders, so useful in moments of stress,
that life's delights come mostly luck
or grace anyway, e.g., eyes full-color
gazing straight from the heart.

LETTER TO MY LANDLADY

Dear Eva,

   In your house everything
works: hot runs hot and cold runs cold and
what needs to go down goes directly
down—you never hesitate. You told me
there's nothing much up here, but
what about these windows? I count
fourteen; all of them open, close, and
lock and the screens slide up and down on
fourteen different views of trees, roofs
with chimneys smoking, paths crisscrossing
to school, Mary Ann's fence and clothespin
bag, and at 1:15 the mailman's cap
turning. The bed accommodates me like
the countryside this village sleeps in, as do
twenty-nine hooks per closet—every room
has its big closet. And I cannot believe
your smooth-springing ironing board.

          True
your knives are what you said, dull, but I see
you laugh through what you can't cut. Nor do
the cups match any of the saucers. Yet, vision-
imbalanced myself, I stand to admire
your various resources, like the one mirror
giving me the top half and the other,
the other—well, the full picture of me
lording around your abundant house, that's
more than you could take in all at once
anyway. So here's the rent again.

LETTER #2 TO MY LANDLADY

Dear, dear Eva,
                      Time hangs
so heavy on my hands. In my mind
I'd built another house for you—doors and
windows the same and the cool grey
shower curtain and the cupboard
full of borrowed dishes; food still
not so hot—cold pizza, burnt toast, coffee
way too strong, but you climbing my stair
calling hello from the bottom and bringing
Mrs. Smith defrosted.

I never saw you go, didn't hear you
turn a knob, the latch did not click.
You must have waved goodbye to your clocks
ticking and chiming deep in your
gold carpets and just floated away from all warm
ample houses on earth. Where

are you living now? If I came there, homeless again
and with almost no money to speak of, could we
make another little arrangement, so when I turned out
my light, yours across the driveway would still be
winking way up through the night leaves?

CO-EXISTENCE

Music, which is usually considered
the most time-bound of the arts, is
the transformation of time into space.
—Source unknown

The minute the first
trumpet of the Second
Brandenburg scored the air,
that Dalmatian beyond my window
bounded free of the leash and
at full gallop, spots afire, tail
high as a baton, tore off
around the pond, whirling old Bach
into reaches of space
until then empty of time.

SUMMER CAN TAKE YOU

In her picture of June the child
has painted herself already
a good inch higher than the old fellow
who leans on his cane, watching.
Looking neither right nor left, but
inward, not seeing the boy
with his bag of potatoes nor the woman
in a headscarf bending into the baby carriage
nor the traffic officer
who sets his bare hands against
two or three cars and the lopsided
school bus, she is holding on tight
to the red and purple umbrella sailing
her and her hair and her blue ruffles up
toward some trees ballooning in green
over the other side of the street. She'll
make it, all right. Her trees need
more swirls, of course, and for herself
we will want to see clearly the delicate upcurve
on her mouth as she floats, but that
will be easy enough because before painting time
draws to a close you catch on to everything,
how it all goes and where
feeling like summer can take you.

MORNING SWIM

Out on the rock
where the yard begins to tip,
an early mist slides in
between your eyes
and all the signs you live by.
You can't put a face on, name
who's on the porch beginning breakfast
or maybe just about to chip
through that old paint
to wood like new.

Clinging to this rim, not seeing
is not knowing, is not being
anything at all except
what's pushing at us so
we shiver up from rock
to feel our way down
deeper, through the creaking
gate to the very bottom of the garden
where the pool lies
clear and sudden as a turquoise eye.

I Climb into My Study

That Water flowing from a rock,
the Bread, the Shepherd's
careless sheep,
all naming words from Adam on,
and seeking words that try
defining swift disclosure,
Him or Her—
the plain fact is
those sturdy words have left me.

Tongue-tied together with today,
seeing the hammock's empty
I climb into my study of at least
how one loosed breath's enough
to open many-layered leaves like fans
on blue designs I've never seen before;
how something low and near at hand will rustle,
out of nowhere something trill,
and shadows shift; or clouds, for instance,
how they roil or float or spill
through someone's fingers weaving here and now
into forever as a silence starts to hum
and how this humming unnamed knowledge I breathe in,
this swaying web, contains me.

III.

Scorched Season

HYMN TO THE BLESSED TREES

1. In the morning I turn first
    to the trees, their green
    thought floating into the light.
    Each tree has its low, steadfast
    beginning in roots that make
    ways for the branches to spread
    leaves soft or crisp
    in their myriad shapes and
    turnings, until at our feet
    lie the blessings of shade quietly woven
    while we were asleep. I welcome the trees
    growing taller morning by morning.

2. I think of the trees, how
    when we pay attention we can see
    their singular distress. With greater
    or lesser oozing of sap, they
    counteract our lawnmowers and dull
    saws and recover sometimes and
    forgive us. Birds weave song
    among them with who knows what
    healing influence, yet I owe apology
    to the willow for yesterday's crude
    attack on the branches. I find myself
    in this scorched season unworthy
    of the patient, daily trees.

3. Passing below with my book bag
    I continue to feel drawn by the trees'

soft insistence to reach high
into the meaning of the earth and
over the earth, to swim
through their green rustling
as branch after branch hands me higher
into new designs at the top,
because stretching my trunk and arms
could bring to the trees
another five feet of height and breadth,
besides names of categories outer and
inner, including all possible
categories of desire.

4.   Inside the building I
resist the metaphor the trees suggest
but it returns unabashed
to impose simplicity and
directness upon me when beyond
my one window the pond lies full
of the mirroring of leaves.

5.   What is the language of trees, and why
do its syllables bid my eye number first
their general shapes coning,
ballooning high fans, then their particular
tensions of strength from the center
along two or three twigs and stems to
one light-spattered leaf where the cicada
over and over is counting? Number
leading to dream, and I must begin

once again to enter the trees,
become their cool center, then their root
dividing the dark before rising and branching
over the lawn and the people as if
abiding forgiveness were all we can do.

6.   A dear gift from the trees, when we
can receive it, this telling us darkness
and light are the same. Their branch systems
mirror their root systems so faithfully
that paying attention we discover in blue- or
yellow-green outspreading of leaves how
fares the deepest heart of the tree. Their being
and their language are the same. Of what
other system can this much be said?

7.   This asking, and the stand of elm
coming halfway toward home,
I prop myself against
their rough truth, trusting
the leaves as if noticing
will hush their twigs and branches back
down into dark-
dividing roots, easing
my own return to forgiveness
spreading shade over this scorched
season and finding me once again blessing
the patient, daily families of trees.

MIDWAY BETWEEN

Faces, too, midway
between flowers and stars: we want to
understand everything, thinking of them.

SUGGESTION

How would it be if,
before it's too late,
you came a bit closer,
from behind, wearing
your old blue work shirt
open down the front
so I could
back into it
and slide my arms
all the way
down the sleeves
past the cuffs and
you could help me
button it up
with you and me in it?
That way, from then on
I'd be wrapping
my arms around
whatever you wrap
your arms around and
things would be better.

I Buy an Old Picture for Emily's Baptismal Day

From a pear wood frame smaller than a postcard
the child looks out, white-slippered feet
pointed in place beneath her pantalets. But
a dark sort of work apron pulled askew
over the white dress tells us
she's been at filling the basket on her arm—and
sure enough, we see what seems one new
white egg already gathered in; her other
arm luminous in its white sleeve,
she is about to pick a rambler rose just
grown into her reach.
                        Standing still busy
against a background of brown time, she has
something to say I grope for,
but Emily will know. Placing her own
small feet this day in timelessness, she
will know and, when I ask, tell me in her way
why some child at a burgeoning rose tree
must stand always gathering in as we gaze
back at a time when we, too, set out,
our brand-new selves, with our baskets.

WITH REFERENCE TO STARS

Out here in fly-over country
one night I read your poems
aloud to myself. Some poems
were like on top of a hill
and a person you know
is quietly naming the stars.

Then again,
in the Bible it says
there was a time when
the morning stars laughed together.
What on earth about? you might
ask. How half the time
we wouldn't see them or even
know they were there? how
we would reach for them
anyway? visit them uninvited
or breeze by? Were they already
that long ago laughing at
what we would name them?

WHAT WE KNOW

Trying to keep what we know
to ourselves, trying
not to,
        we notice
the bare field, how it points
toward a target of doves brooding
on flight, although for the moment
they bunch motionless
within a space of cold defined for them
by the branches through which
we are looking.
                Only a dozen or so leaves
remain on the tree. It is easy
to count one leaf, then another, as they
drop away in a pattern by now
familiar.
                When two or three raisins
burnt in the baking fall
into the path of the broom, even this
reminds us of something.
                        At the same time, over
several days pairs of hands, not always
the same hands, pick up the flowering
cactus, carrying it
setting it down letting it probe
room after shadowed room with light.

ALMOST THAT LONG

Next morning that woman,
tower of anger,
took knife
to her flower bed still
blooming in spite of the frost,
brought in fistfuls, then
drove them one by one
into a narrow-necked vase
ridiculously fluted. This
she planted between us
to cancel out my face
and hide hers from mine.
I was given to see only
her mums day after day, a
washed-out lavender I'd never
choose for myself. She kept a close
watch: let one droop, start
wrinkling down, she was there
with a fresh one. For almost two
weeks her plan held. It takes
almost that long: a glance,
one-eyed, across opening space, a
ventured softness
at the mouth, then her rough
fingers touched mine as I
handed my dishes into the sink.

THREE CATS

Malt and Strider in a poised meander
down the six-foot fence: eight paws place,
with what grace, their pointed progress
halfway to the swings, brushing past
sunflower heads, to let them know.

They choose exalted ways, gravity
be hanged, dole out quite aerial judgments
with the merest twitch toward
damp spots, tight spots, garbage cans,
have much to think about.

But Claude: I had not made
one song for him before he died.
He sulked in corners, swiped his mother's face;
barred from the supper dish, he took his meals
alone, by the lilac bush.

Yet for all that, stuck close to home,
but never touch him. Kept such distance
no one missed him, only puzzled over
Malt and Strider pouncing on each other,
restless, mewing, nudging at his bush.

Without a proper dirge will we forget
this scrawny stiffness lifted from decay
to decent burial that day? Strider and Malt
have since resumed their walks and peace
prevails, and larger, knowing,
unarticulated grief.

TWO POTS OF IVY

Two pots of ivy: one
choked with leaves; the other
casting a long stem, leaf
here and there gathering space.

           They don't
speak, just
bide the same hours
under the same light.

THE POSTCARD

When the face of this earth is no longer smiling
prisms of light around, so much grey air
opens up between objects that
legs of tables and chairs, for instance,
don't know what to do with themselves
anymore: just to stand there
knee-deep in their own shadow seems not quite
enough. Everywhere, the simplest things, even forks,
with nary a glint back from a knife
on the other side of the plate, lose their inventiveness,
think they won't make it up and down one more time
on their own, up and down. So much
unoccupied grey, these objects after a while
drift farther apart from each other, then
away from their words. Then words amble off
one by one and thoughts go shapeless, half-guessing
there won't be a party, only hot-dish again.

How can you do this to us,
when a mere postcard
from your end of the room, a postcard
you breathed on, your breath crystalline-gold-
turquoise-azure-indigo-violet-amethyst, would suffice?

UNDER THE SNOW

Under the snow falling in veils
countless new thoughts are gathering themselves
for discovery, practicing in their mind's eye
proofs, points, the elasticity of reach toward one
soft burst into the open, who will be first? although
likely, some few will need to dream longer and
deeper, still whispering what it could possibly mean.

Do they down there think themselves anything at all
out of the ordinary, their moments of arrival
clean as a whistle through mud and dead leaves
cause for amazement? or do they take it for granted
their inventions will effect contrary traffic,
their stunts and feints distract even themselves
for a time? What is the pleasure
that always shows on their faces?

And what happens next? Well,

countless small thoughts would like simply
to go south. Although clusters of them
by long-standing, if tacit, agreement
get themselves into glass vases on tables
so the erstwhile impoverished air
can hover, a humming aureole, all night long,
most hope at best they'll be strewn by some hand
over warm afternoon-fields of sleep
where the white moth now and then skims,
stirring even the shyest among them
to a last fragrance of the garden
that once shone on their faces.

LIVING HERE

Living here higher than ever,
I see how it'd be possible
to, like, let go,
south wind lifting green-gold
into blue, me breast-stroking
around rustle and snag,
getting the hang of it, Vivaldi or
someone like that cheering me on
past only a minute ago, when I was almost
too old—three flights up plus
groceries and all—for this
very sunny height, true, but now
all at once not very light,
not high enough.

THIS GIRL

She sat there
reading her essay
on the stone wall
with her feet in the garden
nothing showed yet
it is too early for anything
to show in the garden but
she herself wouldn't have cared
where her feet were
she was that intent on polishing
her essay between puffs on
her cigarette which is not
good for her why on earth
does she do that the toes of her small
black shoes side by side
scarcely showed in the dirt
and I thought how she is
her own secret I tried to see
over her shoulder
but her shoulders had a
stillness about them
curled into such
listening
in touch with I saw
roots their feet sure
soundless how they
go after and get there.

EMILY'S VISIT

Emily's visit at best
is a delicate balance.
On the rebound
she lets fly
one yelp then another
to catch, by the merest
chance,
my empty hand.

Her new trick is
this: stand up,
put your head on the rug
no matter what anyone says, then
see how it looks upside down
through your legs, then
push yourself over, who
cares? and
there you are
flat on your back
resting.

I dig into the refrigerator,
tossing out
possibilities for lunch:
mac 'n' cheese
cheese on bread, stew, juice
milk carrots celery.
Luckily, under
my elbow, she spots
grapes.

In the course of her nap
we discuss somersaults. She
will teach her brother
as soon as he's two and
not so dumb.
"You can't imagine!" she says,
seizing
yesterday's funnies.

It doesn't matter
that these face her
upside down. It's clear
what she'd like for the moment
is time simply to study them out
undisturbed by more
orderly arrangements of blankets.

Which, of course, are all right but,
like great aunts,
in their place.

TIME AS WHAT WE SEE, HEAR, AND REMEMBER

Time as
what we see, hear, and remember: sparrows,
four or five, follow a line
back and forth east to west branch to feeder.
Yesterday was the same. I sat
in first light only an instant before
light began to be stolen
inch by inch back into evening, watch:
at the field's far edge
nine houses mark a line where
a perceivable slant moving east to west
shortens the shadow under each gable.
I could measure the whole story in sparrows
rushing their sharp diagonal.

Listen, besides: notations of chirps
press through the glass room after room
to join deep-flowing sleep, each sleeper
her own rhythm, all our lives simply
stealing away.

This dark thieving: when the child
in her car seat closes her eyes,
is time even then acquainting her blood
with revolutions per minute
ribboning on down side streets toward
the familiar-feel soft slowing
near the end, and someone lifting her dream
back down a long hallway, loosening

this mitten then that
then the cap tied close under her chin,
leaving the pulse and the unbooted small foot
flung finally free?

By some design I am drawn back
to embrace mother, foot caught at the curb,
grandmother caught at the shore,
great-grandmother crumpled into a ditch,
staring into the passage of time. My father
recedes down the track, his thin shoulders
pulling my heart along through trolley doors
clanging behind him.

SMALL TALK

At the playground
the children learn stretching, sliding,
swinging, plunging, ropes, chutes, chains.
They don't use all these words, yet
everyone's shrieking at once.

On the sidelines, leaning in from the railing,
a handful of babysitters in a position
to interpret call out directions
and cautions, judgments, praise, make
stern accusations.

In no position to judge, four or five daisies
(weeds, really) nod in the breeze
and the pansies look shrewd
in case they ought to be listening,

while out of nowhere, out of the blue
scoops of cloud ready to burst
nudge down closer
into line with the river
everyone knows is full of and, what's more,
getting away with, its own story.

Rescue Party in Kansas

Everything flattened after the deluge.
Then down the street from my window,
her Sunday dress a piece of sky
rippling over the grass,
her hair a small cloud floating,

one by one they cross
to where the blue van waits
in the sun in somebody's driveway,
sidestep puddles gutters lost branches
she careful for her covered dish
he hitching up a couple of bulky sacks
and a blanket
each child swinging her plastic bag
hopping where necessary
the old man in coveralls last
dragging his right foot a little
carrying only a long life
willing to listen.

POEM AS LANDSCAPE

White as far as I can see,
except words, two or three
black and fat swoop down
to waddle around, peck at
nothing but white
before moving on and
who wouldn't? I suppose
they left tracks.

Something to go on.

I see whatever I'm breathing
blue-grey at the edges,
breath Two pushing breath One
higher into the air. Just air.

All there is.

Poems that start out all airy
lose themselves fast, no backbone,
no sense of direction
except down, in soft terraces,
toward what without too much of a stretch
could be a pond buried deep under there
and an island of sorts
with a wood bench near a green tree
where one could sit quite a while in the sun
and stare down at fishes coming and going
smooth as sentences one two three.

If it were summer.

For the most part
this poem is still winter,
I can tell. Well.

Up ahead six to six
Brewberry's will feed me.

ON GIVING UP

I gave up Negative Remarks for Lent.
It took the whole first week
for me to grasp
this single imperfection.
But then it came,
served up on its little platter
neat as an omelet "NO VIA NEGATIVA
FOR SIX WEEKS. TRY IT,
YOU'LL LIKE IT."

Indeed, it sobers me
to hear myself complain:
I rise to praise all sun and water
flowing over rock, seek out wine
to go with pasta. And wit—
I'll never have enough of wit,
it radiates good vibes.

And yet, re sober thoughts:
what's wrong with *no*, *not*, *isn't*,
never will? They have their truth:
God said, I AM, but
so am I,
and I'm not God. Nor,
as far as I can see,
is any other name now known:
God IS but thrives on being ISN'T,
and in just such terrifying,
non-affirming ways as ours,

who probe the dark, then stumble,
then cry out in heaps of helplessness.

I ponder thus on Thursday of Week Six.

Change of Venue While Waiting for Godot

For Sale or, that failing,
give-away:

>one nicked brass pot for spraying plants
>>(breathe lovingly on all leaves)

>a can of rocks
>>(fast held in their secrets forever)

>one felt Xmas stocking
>>(really, now)

>a Mexican moth pinned in a plastic box
>>(grieve for victims of beauty)

>candles: two red, like Xmas tree bulbs, plus brass holders;
>two white, honeycombed; one bayberry; third red on a tinfoil
>disc
>>(burn deeper in a dark world)

>this chunk of amethyst someone delved and delivered
>>(deeper, even, than purple)

>three gilt angels singing Hosanna
>>(I cannot believe their faces and small pointed feet)

>Camus and Gide
>>(these, too, I no longer believe)

a coral sponge from Puerto Rico, a dried blowfish from Captiva
      (life is no long resort)

one mug from Tintagel, one glass dragon from Hong Kong,
one hand-carved ballpoint from Thailand
      (why, when the Global Village is within you?)

The Meaning of Art and *Long Day's Journey into Night*
      (something here sounds redundant)

THE LILAC BUSH

Every year for years
a lilac bush filled the world
outside my window. Every spring
it rose purple and complete
to meet me, came so close
I reached to breathe the whole full
mass of it in, loneliness
finally a lie.

They cut it down, of course, but somehow,
in a way you wouldn't expect of lilacs
(so wholeheartedly homespun, so guileless),
it rescued itself from the axe and
took to the air higher and faster
than I am turning out to be, sure
of what it was then and is now.

THE ULTIMATE

Looking out on the trees from here
I say that up or down, despite
a tendency to toss and thrash, they all
grow into silence, the sonnet of old age:
roots fold around, feel through the quiet dark,
pass their likeness by without a word
but all of one mind to sink still deeper,
easefully, making their simple seeking prayer;
if here and there along the way a syllable gets dropped,
no matter—what's done needed to be done. Roots
have their wisdom.
                          As do branch and leaf: I note
how through their growing seasons
they separate themselves from clusters
to tend more singly upward into light—the wide,
deep, open arms of light. Who wouldn't,
entered here, leave off all words?
My own heart at the thought
would hide itself this instant still as death
within the wide, deep, open arms of light.

As for the shaft-like middle ground of trees,
trunk line of rhyme and reason—be it blest
as necessary phase. The ultimate in song
is silence, dark and light.

IV.

The Turning Page

I KNOW THE BODY IN ITS NARROW BED

I know the body
narrow-wed
to slants and knobs
and realignments under scars. I
meet its eyes, their outsized hollows
making promises to none except
a coming nakedness, and watch
as one by one the dignities
bow out and it is left
to sift into its own secret, wait
for its fruit—
                for resurrection
is another's business:
                    I am that mere sigh
of all the earth, clasping the body
longer in a lesser love.

THE IRIS

The iris, the cool
cup of it, fills
every morning

as we wake, its
tongued light
a language—

inside, I mean—
rising sea-
blue to purple
to wine.

THE TOAD

There's a crack in the brick
where the wall meets a step by the back door.
A toad lives there.
First time, he hopped out of my way. But not far,
being at home in his body.

I come along mornings to collect rent
or something, look for at least eyes
in that soft heap of bumps.

He may be asleep, rear end packing the crack,
chin and throat—no difference—almost flat
against the grey carpet but fluttering, to himself.
Or you, even. Toad talk.

In the moist quiet you lean closer, listen,
take note, know very well but not why
you've been called to record him.

SHIFT

But a shift
shower of gold
down blue so
the heart flies
to its doorway,
arms wide to
vast coming
intentions a
rustle a leaf
lying like light.

CATNESS

Strider the cat and I have this in common:
two days now we've been without
the lady of the house, who takes off far too often
and for good, as far as cat experience has it,
anyway. Which is to say,
when she roams whining, whipping her tail and,
as she did last night, leaps wild-eyed
to the windowsill, she's all but lost
in catness.

This morning, then, when she emerged
early, wet to the knees, from the sumac
where I trust she'd fought another night alone
and, catching sight of me,
set up that howl again no cat food
in the shape of stars can satisfy,
I took her on my lap.

I had come searching too, so waited
while she probed in circles for a feel of home,
pointing her chin here and then there
into the sun along my knee until
at last, heavy with purrs, her eye-
lids slowly sealed. And so did mine,
on crickets weaving what seemed hymns
of cats and people dreaming into one.

LATE SKETCHES

This late October sun
lays shadows of a few last
gingko leaves
against my wall,
designs so intricate
the eye assumes a new regard
for what's not really
there except
obliquely and
at some remove, in
patterns at our back

as of some
fingertip or lip
now long beyond desire
or school of thought loose-
brushing past,
a kind of aftersong
whose name escapes us.

BACKYARD

Low sun
feels its way down
through yellowing birch
to touch up asters
impatiens zinnias
and a tangle
of red berries
one more time
before it leaves us
sitting so
dreamily fingering
almonds and
an amber drink.

THE DANCER

I saw the dancer in the sky.
She filled the whole sky and
that whole day the old pike hung
in green light at the edge
of the pond watching. Free
over the air she moved, gliding
her hair down the low hills, now
her arm lifting a webbed sleeve
past her cheek, now a wisp
of gown sweeping her hip
to her toe spinning
in space. Once
in a white light she came
bending her knee toward us in the stubble
and all my blood rose into that moment
I thought I could run with the dancer
into the sky: sifted by singing
no one could hear, we would fill
the whole air. But a small coolness
touched her and she soared
taller and higher away. That was when
I turned to my cat, who blinked
but said nothing, for neither my cat
nor the crickets morning to night nor I,
certainly, had ever seen anything like
this goddess over the earth
and us on it, playing
the blue light between. Filling our eyes
with her dancing, we had filled up the whole day.

WORLD LIT

September crickets
heavy with heat. Our task being
World Lit, we will begin with
Odysseus. Without much hope
for shared dispositions,

try to
imagine yourself back
from swimsuits on TV
to seas churning up terrible
monsters: for a long time now
we've had real monsters and faced
striking out on our own
over a broiling sea, right?
the distance between him and us
not all that great
               on and on
meeting briefly now and then.

Toward the end, goodness
caught us up the mountain
lightening ledge by ledge some
thing of darkness bit by bit until
no essays left, nor words, only
this final meeting I acknowledge mine.

AN ANCIENT VISION

—on a feast of Mary

An ancient vision has
the woman laboring in childbirth
while a dragon close by
lashes stars with its tail.

The child, her one son, snatched up
into God just in time, the woman
escapes to the desert and is fed there
some twelve-hundred-fifty-odd days.

This morning
the widows came streaming out
from the shadowy church, two dozen or so
helping each other along
down the block toward the apartments.

Pilgrims, I thought,
like that woman who lived in the desert.

MOUNTAIN MEADOW

Let the poor pilgrim dream,
for pillow a stone.
In far finer air sing
grasses and daisies: listening,
the white moth skims.

WIDOW

Dawn came. Love's
floor swept
deep as death,
I lean on my broom now,
wanting your word.

Webs, whispers,
how they cling!

Distance is
cloudbank
spindrift a
whistle a sport
tasting of brine.

Some fires burn
deeper even
than death.

Would you agree?

My treasure, my
one heart wordless
adrift toward its harbor,
where are you? I am here
in the doorway of night.

TO COME SO

O holy One
I am ashamed
to come so
full of words: every
flower and its stem,
the rushing
multiple light
interweaving with grasses,
and how the sand
slides my feet down
over a scatter of shells
closer. Pity
my loose tongue crying
your name even
as I turn my mouth
into the fragrance
of your hand
at my cheek. Save me
then, hear only
a thousand birds
flying over.

Hunter Out of the Dawn

When leaves crisp, when hoarfrost catches the throat,
then hunters, bold under bright stars, get up,
pack their guns and push down to the dock.

Early on such a day my father, too,
hunting a special prize, said his good-byes
in our arms and went out into the dawn.
He went alone, undaunted. Having heard
some time before how this was to be done,
he took with him no gun.

Now he is gone. But in his face
I found the Father of us all—
sweet Life and Providence, Hero bold ranging,
Hunter out of the dawn.

I HAD THOUGHT IT WAS LOST

I had thought it was lost
over that wild field of snow
somewhere, I cannot remember,
I set out to cross one lone afternoon:

the song began there, then rose
in vast drifts somewhere in me
so vast, I remember, we sang together
what I had never before heard
nor could then understand, on and on,
asking neither breath nor understanding,
forgetting how easily ungoverned song
can lose itself to darkening air
long before fields finally end and lights
at the edge signal voices of home.

All that I scarcely remembered—except now,
walking deeper past late light,
vast drifts again in me rising, I understand
no song flung from dark into dark
but moves free, justified and forever
belonging where love's longing
has flung it.

O my dear,
we fly so loose in the wind!

I watch the willow from my rocker,
nod with it, glad the heater's purring at my feet.

Whistler's Mother in her time sat
held together at the top by her lace cap
and at the bottom by the tips of two black shoes;
midway and furthermore, her hands sat
folded in her lap.

In another time, in another chair placed like a pew,
and getting stronger by the day,
I came alone and all at once within the world's
night sky, its vast uncomprehended wilds
springing as far as I could see with stars
and planets attuned to one another's distances
by songs I couldn't hear. But my breath and blood
knew they were singing.

I had no floor, no foothold, only eyes enough to see
something—a half-inch shaving—something
lit by a different light
far out there dodging in and out
among those stars, not touching any one
of them, not singing either on its solitary course,
and very small. And all the planets laughed.

I felt their ripple as a shudder of relief
to see me held, together with the stars,
within a single gaze in such immensity of dark.

POST-DILUVIAL

Awash in old descriptions of a world
where everything has been, my name
woke brightly from the deep, a rainbow
flung against containment
traveling her broad arc
toward wonders altogether flame
beyond this bottleful of time.

OVERHEARD: #2

Then God said:

This wooden top shaped like a strawberry
is for cheering me up. It's faded to pink
with blue leaves and specks of white
supposedly straw, and it's chipped
here and there but still definitely
a strawberry. I'm fond of it: the tip
is worn down from so much spinning—which is,
of course, when it's most glorious: one flick
and out it goes on the Grand Tour
of my domain, humming along, curving
past this and that before settling, poised
into its center, spots and leaves now spinning
a rainbow around it. You admire and admire—
such fierce ease of performance, making its point
with such confident grace on and on.

*

When comes next
the barely perceptible swerve, the lurch oops!
then wobble, tipping a bit this time,
touching the ground flat now but still
to and fro on its roundness,
now simply stopped,
every chip and spot showing,
I've learned I must let it rest
for as long as it wants to,
I'm that fond of it.

OF THE SPIRITS

Three found me sapphires
for eyes to bless
even small fish, their secret
darting and gliding.

Two found for me fire
in stone, wine-dark
purple folded
in purple.

One holds the sun.

One
I am told
kneels unto the end
before the throne of beginnings.

EVENSONG

Flows the wide river.
Soon will rise
nighthawks and fireflies,
steeple, bell
tower, new moon
and evening star—sapphire,
the turning page.

MARY VIRGINIA MICKA, Professor Emerita of English, the College of St. Catherine, St. Paul, Minnesota, is a Sister of St. Joseph of Carondelet, St. Paul Province. Over the years she has published several chapbooks of her poetry and prose and has read from her work frequently. She has conducted numerous retreats and workshops and is currently a member of the Carondelet Center for Spirituality in St. Paul.

She traces her interest in the craft of poetry to her first encounter with the iambic pentameter in sixth grade, when she saw how language can be used not only to identify and define, but also to catch the pace, the color, the very *feel* of the world around and within us—everything from delight to despair, from abandonment to absolution to a blest and wordless peace. The poems in this collection are among her many attempts to get that whole feel figured out for herself, if not for generations to come.

This is the first
book produced by
Ytterli Press. It is set in a
beautiful classic typeface called
Künstler, designed by the German
typographer Georg Trump (1896–1985). It
is especially suitable for poetry due to its high
readability, shapely letters, and timeless feel. In old
Norwegian, *ytterli* is a place-name designating the "outer
fields" of a large farm; it is the original family name of
Sylvia Ruud, designer of this book. In modern
Norwegian, it can also mean "far out," "outly-
ing," or "still more"! This fits with the
purpose of Ytterli Press, which is
to publish works of merit that
may not fall within the
purview of the ordi-
nary outlets for
publish-
ing.